AF480795

LEWIS PUBLISHING

The Long Journey Home

A Road to Redemption and Acceptance

By

Wes Lewis

Published by Lewis Publishing, an imprint of Lewis Strategic Group LLC.

This is a work of nonfiction based on the author's experiences. Names, details, and identifying characteristics have been changed where necessary to protect privacy.

First Edition

Printed in the United States of America

DEDICATION

This book is dedicated to anyone who has ever felt forgotten, left behind, or without a place they could truly call home.

For those who have watched others seem rooted while you learned to live in motion. For those who have carried invisible wounds that rarely show on the surface but shape every decision underneath. If you are still searching—still carrying burdens you don't always have words for—I wrote this with you in mind.

It is also dedicated to those I hurt along the way. I was often lost, struggling to understand my own pain, and my actions reflected that confusion. In trying to survive my own battles, I sometimes created new ones for others. I carry responsibility for it now, fully and without excuse, and I offer this work as part of my continued effort toward accountability and healing.

This book is a work of memoir based on the author's personal experiences, recollections, and reflections. While every effort has been made to present events accurately, certain names, identifying details, and circumstances have been changed to protect the privacy of individuals. Some dialogue and timelines may be reconstructed or condensed from memory.

The perspectives expressed in this book represent the author's personal understanding of events and should not be interpreted as definitive accounts of the actions, intentions, or experiences of others.

This book is not intended to provide medical, psychological, legal, or professional advice. The author shares personal experiences related to trauma, recovery, and personal growth for informational and reflective purposes only. Readers seeking professional guidance should consult qualified professionals appropriate to their individual circumstances.

SPECIAL THANKS

I would like to extend my sincere gratitude to the songwriters, musicians, record labels, and fans behind the songs that serve as chapters throughout this book. During some of the most difficult periods of my life, these songs gave me language when I had none and steadiness when I felt untethered. They filled quiet rooms during long nights when sleep would not come, and they traveled with me through unfamiliar cities where I often felt both anonymous and exposed.

The ability to reflect on my journey and document the final year of my travels would not have been possible without the music that carried me through it. These works mean more to me than I can adequately express, and I will forever be grateful for what you created.

I am also deeply thankful to the authors whose books I read—and often reread—while traveling and working through my personal demons. Many of those pages were turned in hotel rooms, airport terminals, and quiet corners of coffee shops where I sat alone trying to make sense of my own life. At some of the lowest points in my journey, your words helped me stand back up, put down the bottle, and believe that a different path was still possible.

For a long time, discouragement nearly extinguished my desire to create, but your work reignited my passion for writing and helped guide me back toward a productive life. I owe you more than you will ever know.

Finally, I would like to thank the men and women of Waffle House Store #1073 for the countless mornings fueled by Diet Coke, a perfectly made All-Star meal, and genuine kindness. Those mornings were often quiet ones. I would sit in the same booth, sometimes before the sun had fully risen, watching the steady rhythm of customers coming and going while I tried to steady my own thoughts.

Your consistency, warmth, and simple acts of care mattered more than you could have known. A smile and a sincere "good morning" can carry someone further than you might imagine—especially when they may look okay on the outside but are quietly struggling within.

Contents

INTRODUCTION

I learned early that home was temporary.

Before I turned eleven, my family moved so often that packing boxes were never fully unpacked. They stayed stacked in corners, flattened against walls, borrowed by neighbors who knew we would need them again soon. Sometimes they still smelled faintly of tape and cardboard dust, reminders that nothing in our lives was meant to settle for long. I learned to recognize the sound of packing tape being pulled tight across a box before I learned how to recognize the feeling of stability.

One year, we moved six times—six addresses, six first days, six sets of neighbors who learned our names just as we were leaving. Each move required starting over in small but exhausting ways: learning new bus routes, new classroom layouts, new social rules that seemed already established long before I arrived. In a small town in Kentucky in the 1980s, that kind of movement made you memorable for the wrong reasons. People noticed the child who never stayed long enough to become familiar. I learned how to say goodbye before I learned how to stay.

What I didn't learn was how to belong.

Even then, I understood something was off—not in the dramatic way children articulate pain, but in the quiet way they adapt. Children rarely announce what hurts them; they adjust instead. I learned not to get attached to places. I learned not to need too much. I learned that stability was something other families had—something that seemed permanent and ordinary for them, but distant and unpredictable for me. Affection was something that arrived sparingly and left without notice. No one was cruel. No one was malicious. But love was rarely spoken aloud, and physical affection came so infrequently that I can still count the times my mother hugged me as a child.

I don't say this to assign blame. I say it because it explains everything that came after.

By the time I was an adult, motion felt normal. Stillness felt dangerous. Remaining in one place long enough to examine my own thoughts created a kind of discomfort I didn't yet understand. When the opportunity to leave came—when the military offered structure, purpose, and a reason to keep moving—I took it without hesitation. The decision felt natural, almost inevitable, as if my entire childhood had quietly been preparing me for a life defined by relocation.

Over the next twenty-five years, I lived all over the world, often relocating every two years with the precision of a metronome. Orders would arrive, timelines would be set, and within weeks I would be packing once again—this time with military efficiency instead of childhood uncertainty. I built a career. I earned degrees. I rose in rank. From the outside, my life looked like the American promise fulfilled: a poor Black kid made good through discipline and sacrifice.

Inside, something was eroding.

I married. I divorced. I married again. I divorced again. I became a father and tried, consciously, to give my children what I didn't have—consistency, affection, reassurance. I wanted to create the stability I had never known. In many ways, I succeeded. In other ways, I fell short in ways that would take years to fully understand. I did some of it well. Other parts I failed spectacularly. I told myself the failures were temporary, the costs necessary, the damage manageable. I learned how to perform competence while quietly avoiding the work of reckoning.

By forty-two, I had achieved most of what I was taught to want—and yet I was unraveling.

I drank too much. I worked too hard. I carried anger like a companion and justified it as stress. I chased validation in places I already knew would not satisfy me. Professional success became a shield that allowed me to avoid confronting deeper questions about identity, purpose, and emotional stability. I was respected professionally and hollow personally. The irony was not lost on me: I had spent decades preparing for every mission except the one that mattered most— learning how to live with myself when the uniform came off.

Retirement didn't free me. It exposed me.

Without schedules to hide behind and expectations to meet, the questions I had postponed began asking themselves. The structure that had once organized my days was gone, and in its absence, silence grew louder. Who was I without motion? What did home mean to someone who had never stayed long enough to find it? And why, after a lifetime of service and sacrifice, did I feel so profoundly untethered?

I didn't set out to travel the world to find answers. I didn't have a master plan or a spiritual blueprint. I left on what can only be described as a half-formed idea: go back to the places where I had almost felt content and see if any of them could hold me now. It wasn't a dramatic decision. It was quiet, tentative, and uncertain— much like the internal questions that had been growing for years.

I moved by road, air, and sea, covering more than sixty thousand miles in a year. Airports blurred together. Train stations became familiar landscapes of movement and transition. I slowed down in ways I never had before. I listened. I paid attention. I allowed myself to feel what I had spent decades suppressing.

Along the way, I confronted truths I would have preferred to avoid— about addiction, identity, faith, failure, and the quiet damage of never settling. I met people who mirrored parts of myself I hadn't named yet. Some encounters were brief but profound. Others were uncomfortable reflections of patterns I had carried for years. I also discovered that healing is not a revelation; it is a practice. It requires honesty, patience, and a willingness to sit with discomfort without rushing to resolution.

This book is not a guide. It is not a prescription. It is not an argument that travel, service, or discipline will save you. This journey was mine. Yours will look different. What I offer here is not advice, but testimony—an account of what happens when a man stops running long enough to listen to his own life.

The Long Journey Home is the story of searching for belonging in a world that taught me how to leave, of confusing movement with meaning, and of discovering—slowly, imperfectly—that home is not a destination you arrive at, but a condition you build. Sometimes that construction requires tearing things down first.

I am still learning. I am still accountable for what I broke along the way. But for the first time in my life, I am not in a hurry to depart.

This is where the journey begins.

CHAPTER 1

Starting Over

I had been wasting away in a prison of my own making for more than three months, and the worst part was that I couldn't even tell you exactly when the prison door had closed. There had been no single dramatic moment—no event you could circle on a calendar and say, that's when everything changed. One day I was functioning—moving, answering emails, handling responsibilities— and the next I was living inside a house that felt like a holding cell. I had no plan to snap out of it. No momentum. No clear reason that explained why I couldn't just stand up and be who I used to be.

For the first time in my life, there was no schedule waiting for me. No uniform to put on. No one briefing me on the day's mission. No children's activities to coordinate. No phone calls I had to return. No crisis that required my leadership. The noise that had filled my life for decades had gone quiet, and in the quiet, I discovered something I hadn't been prepared for.

My own mind was louder than anything outside the walls.

It replayed conversations I wished I had handled differently. It replayed mistakes with perfect clarity. It asked questions I had avoided for years. Without external demands to distract me, there was nowhere left to hide from my own thoughts.

I remember lying on the bathroom floor, staring at the edge of the tub like it was the only thing holding the room in place. The tile was cold against my cheek, and that coldness felt strangely grounding, as if it were the only physical sensation cutting through the fog in my head. My body felt heavy, as if gravity had doubled. Even lifting my arm felt like a task that required more energy than I had available.

The air had that stale, closed-up smell a house gets when curtains stay shut and windows don't open—an unmoving air that felt thick, almost visible. I don't remember how long I had been down there. Time was no longer something I could measure in hours. It was measured in drinks, in nights, in whether I could force myself to stand up long enough to make it to the kitchen.

I had not talked to a single person in two weeks.

That wasn't an exaggeration. I wasn't "keeping to myself." I wasn't "taking some space." I was isolated in a way that felt deliberate, like my body and mind had agreed that distance from everything— including people—was safer than being seen like this. The only voice I heard was the one in my head, and the conversation it kept trying to have with me was one I spent days trying to block out.

Is this where a successful life ends—right here, all alone?

I wasn't dramatic about it. I wasn't searching for attention. I was simply doing the math in real time, the way a man does when he is too tired to lie to himself anymore. My mind kept circling the same questions like a vulture:

How long before someone notices?

How long before someone drives up to the house and knocks on the door?

How many knocks before they realize no one is coming?

Would they call someone? Would the police break the door down?

And then the most ridiculous thought would slide in—because that's how my mind works even when it's collapsing:

Not the front door. I'd have to pay for new locks. A new door. Another expense. Another embarrassing moment.

That's the kind of warped logic that exists when you're in deep trouble. Even on a bathroom floor, even while contemplating ending your life, part of my mind was still trying to control outcomes— still trying to manage consequences—still trying to keep the optics clean. The instinct to maintain order, to anticipate fallout, to solve logistical problems—even in a moment of emotional collapse—had been trained into me for decades.

But the truth was simpler than all my thoughts.

I was drinking too much, and I couldn't stop.

One drink led to the next drink, and the next bottle, and the next night. What had once felt like a way to unwind after long days had quietly shifted into something else entirely. I told myself I was going through a phase. I told myself I just needed to take the edge off. I told myself I had earned it. I told myself I was still in control because I had done hard things in life and I had always found my way through before.

None of that mattered on that floor.

Alcohol doesn't just dull pain. It also dulls perspective. It slowly takes the polite, thoughtful man you believe you are and replaces him with someone you don't recognize—someone whose mouth moves faster than his conscience, someone who is quick to anger, someone who can turn small irritations into explosions. The damage it causes isn't always one big catastrophic moment. Sometimes it's a slow battlefield of hurt feelings and burned bridges. And when you finally look up, you realize the people who matter most have backed away for their own protection.

Lying there, I wondered if anyone would care that I had lived at all.

Would anyone attend my funeral?

Would my children forgive me?

Did they even care?

I hadn't talked to any of them in months. My drinking had alienated me from the rest of the world, and if I'm honest, I had played a role in that alienation. I wasn't only being abandoned. I was also pushing people away—ignoring calls, avoiding conversations, withdrawing from any interaction that might force me to confront the reality of what I had become.

That is a hard truth to write. It was even harder to admit then.

I remember closing my eyes and thinking: if I don't end it today, what happens tomorrow?

Another drink?

Another bottle?

Another night on the floor?

Another day of waking up to the same walls and the same shame?

The house around me was quiet, but it wasn't peaceful. It was a darkness that felt designed to keep me down. It held every memory of what I had built and what I had broken. Everywhere I turned, something reminded me of a version of myself that no longer existed. I didn't feel safe in it. I felt trapped by it—trapped by the weight of expectations I had once met and the distance between that man and who I had become.

And that's when something finally broke through the fog—not hope, not a miracle, not a sudden burst of motivation.

A simple realization:

If I stay here, I'm going to die.

Maybe not immediately. Maybe not dramatically. But I was going to drink myself into an early grave, or I was going to do something reckless enough to hurt myself or someone else, and the end result would be the same.

I didn't need more willpower. I didn't need another speech to myself. I needed a plan—something concrete enough to pull me out of the loop I was stuck inside, something practical enough to interrupt the cycle I could no longer break through thought alone.

Later, I would listen to Chris Stapleton's "Starting Over" on repeat and realize why the song had grabbed me by the collar. It wasn't the romance of the lyrics. It was the simplicity of the idea: the road rolls out like a welcome mat. A better place than the one we're at.

In that moment, on that bathroom floor, I wasn't thinking about a grand journey or a capstone trip or reinvention.

I was thinking about survival.

I didn't know where I was going yet.

But for the first time in months, I knew one thing with absolute clarity:

I could not stay.

REFLECTION:

What stands out most about this beginning isn't the decision to leave—it's how long I believed endurance alone would save me. For most of my life, I measured strength by how much I could carry and how efficiently I could survive. I built emotional armor so early that it eventually felt like safety, even while it slowly isolated me from myself and the people around me.

It wasn't until I retired from the Army that time finally slowed enough for a full self-assessment. What felt like rock bottom in this chapter was not an ending—it was the starting line to a new version of myself.

Even now, when I find myself in emotionally triggering situations, I sometimes think back to how that cold bathroom floor felt against my cheek and thank God that He gave me an open road instead of a closed door. Starting over wasn't an act of escape; it was an acknowledgment that surviving and truly living are not the same. That realization marked the first time I understood that change requires more than persistence—it requires intention.

CHAPTER 2

Homies

I wasn't trying to destroy anything. I was trying to stay numb. Drinking stopped being something I did at the end of the day and started bleeding into everything else. It crept into mornings, into afternoons, into quiet stretches of time when nothing urgent demanded my attention. I still showed up. I still handled what I needed to handle. From the outside, nothing looked broken.

But I was drinking heavier and doing whatever I could to avoid being alone with my own head. Staying still meant getting too close to thoughts I didn't want to deal with, so I stayed moving.

She didn't come in with some dramatic entrance. She was just there. Half my age. Restless. Alive in a way that made me feel less flat. There was an energy around her that contrasted sharply with the heaviness I carried. She didn't ask about my past, and I didn't offer it. That unspoken agreement felt like relief. We stayed in the present—

late nights, no plan, no direction. For the first time in a long time, I didn't feel like I had to be anything specific. I wasn't a retired officer, a father navigating strained relationships, or a man trying to reconcile decades of decisions. I was just someone occupying the same space as someone else who wasn't asking me to explain myself.

The drugs began almost immediately. They didn't just slip in. I welcomed them. I told myself I was experimenting, that after a lifetime of discipline I had earned the right to feel something different. During that time with her, I wasn't drinking, and I used that as proof I was changing. In reality, I had just replaced one addiction with another. She didn't pressure me. She didn't need to. Everything felt stronger around her—conversation, music, touch. Colors seemed sharper. Time seemed to move differently. I told myself I was tapping into another part of who I was. I

never slowed down long enough to ask what it was costing me.

She didn't have a stable place to stay, and I told myself I was helping. I paid for rooms, food, and clothes. From the outside it looked generous. It gave me a sense of usefulness that felt familiar. It felt like I had purpose. But I wasn't saving her. I was keeping her close. Close to me. Close to the drug. Close to the version of myself that didn't have to reflect on anything. I thought we were building something real. We weren't. We were filling gaps in each other—temporary solutions to deeper problems neither of us was ready to confront.

I called her my homie because that's how I justified it—simple and safe. A label that minimized what was actually happening. Being around her made it easier to ignore what was happening. I told myself I wasn't at risk. The truth is I stepped into territory I had never navigated before, and once I was there, I didn't back out. When she moved on, she took the distraction with her. Not the hunger. That stayed. What she left was silence.

The night I realized I couldn't stay where I was, nothing dramatic happened.

No argument.

No phone call.

No intervention.

Just me sitting on the edge of my bed in the dark without anything to drown it out.

The room smelled stale, the air unmoving in a way that made everything feel heavier. Without her and without the influence, I went right back to drinking heavily. The bottle on the nightstand was empty. Another one sat on the floor. My phone buzzed face-down. I knew who it wasn't. That was enough to ignore it.

I hadn't gone anywhere that day. I didn't need to. Everything I was trying to avoid was already sitting in that room with me—memories, regrets, unanswered questions, and the quiet awareness that the distractions I depended on were temporary by design.

I tried to remember the last time I went to sleep without needing something to quiet my mind. A drink. A smoke. Anything.

I couldn't.

That bothered me more than I expected.

By the standards I used to measure myself, I was fine. I paid my bills. I showed up when I had to. I wasn't missing. I wasn't in jail. I was functioning.

But I wasn't solid.

Earlier that evening, I drove to the liquor store without thinking about it. Same route. Same parking spot. Same routine. The familiarity of the pattern was almost comforting in its predictability. I grabbed what I always grabbed. The cashier rang me up without looking at me. We didn't need to acknowledge each other. We both knew why I was there.

That's when it finally settled.

If I stayed like this, nothing dramatic would happen.

I would just slowly narrow.

My world would continue shrinking—fewer conversations, fewer connections, fewer parts of myself engaged with anything beyond survival.

I thought about the version of myself I kept presenting—controlled, capable—and how much energy it took to keep him together.

When the distractions wore off, there wasn't much underneath.

I picked up my phone. My hands weren't panicked. They were steady in a different way. Clear.

I opened my notes app and typed:

I can't stay.

I didn't know where I was going. I didn't have a plan. I just knew staying wasn't neutral for me anymore. It had become active harm.

I went into the bathroom and looked at myself in the mirror. Not long. Just enough.

"You can't fix this here," I said.

There was no argument.

Back on the bed, I opened a flight app. I wasn't looking for somewhere specific. I just needed to see that there were options. Places where I wasn't already known. Places that didn't carry the weight of my recent choices.

It didn't feel exciting.

It felt necessary.

I didn't book anything that night.

But I didn't talk myself out of it either.

When the sun came up, it didn't feel symbolic. It felt like a line had been drawn and I finally saw it.

Later, people would assume I left for freedom or discovery.

I didn't correct them.

The truth was simpler.

I left because I admitted that staying was costing me more than I wanted to admit.

I wasn't running toward something yet.

I was choosing not to keep shrinking.

REFLECTION:

Loneliness was a silent killer for me during that period of my life. For the first time, I had nothing but free time and no established routine to anchor me. I didn't realize how much the structure of the Army had simplified my world until it was gone. I was unprepared for the sudden drop in responsibility, the absence of daily planning, and how deeply I missed the constant problem-solving and strategic thinking that had once defined my days.

So I filled the space with unhealthy habits and surrounded myself with people who reflected where I was emotionally at the time. I am not ashamed of some of the individuals I encountered during that phase. They exposed me to realities I had never experienced before—some good, some destructive, but all instructive. Life is shaped by exposure, and even before I understood I was on a journey, those interactions expanded my perspective.

What I gained most from that period was a deeper appreciation for people who lived differently than I did—those who spoke differently, carried less formal education, or came from circumstances far removed from my own. Being immersed in unfamiliar environments helped me develop a level of empathy and acceptance that later prepared me for emotional challenges I would not have been able to face otherwise.

At the time, I told myself I was choosing my own path. In truth, I was avoiding the vulnerability required for real connection. The distractions I relied on provided temporary relief, but they also kept me from confronting what I was carrying inside.

I did not know it at this point in the journey, but over the course of the coming year, I began to realize that being alone or lonely is not a bad thing. These days, being alone helps me center my thoughts and feelings more constructively.

CHAPTER 3

Son of a Sinner

Before I ever put my car in drive and pointed it toward the coast, I knew that leaving was not going to magically fix anything. I was not naïve enough to believe that geography alone could heal what had taken decades to fracture. Still, I also knew that staying where I was—physically and emotionally—was no longer an option. The journey was not about escape. It was about confrontation.

What I did not anticipate was how much honesty the road would demand from me.

In the early stages of planning—if it could even be called planning—I told myself I was simply starting over. A clean slate. A reset. I did not yet understand that starting over required more than movement. It required me to dismantle the version of myself I had been protecting for most of my adult life.

Travel has a way of stripping away performance. There are long stretches of silence between destinations where there is no one to impress, no role to play, and no routine to hide behind. In those spaces, I was forced to sit with the person I actually was, not the one I thought I had been for twenty-five years.

That reckoning was humbling.

I began to see clearly the ways I had failed the people I loved—not always through cruelty or neglect, but through emotional absence. I had convinced myself that provision was the same as presence, that endurance was the same as love, and that keeping everything moving forward was the same as growth. It wasn't. There were moments in my life when listening would have mattered more than fixing, when patience would have mattered more than discipline, and when vulnerability would have mattered more than control.

I did not arrive at these realizations all at once. They surfaced slowly, often at inconvenient times, usually when I was alone. Every destination peeled back another layer. Each stop forced me to confront pieces of my character I had avoided examining— defensiveness, pride, emotional distance, and a tendency to confuse responsibility with righteousness.

Without that honesty, I would have continued reaching for the same coping mechanisms that had nearly destroyed me. I would have kept drinking, kept numbing, and kept telling myself I was simply going through a phase. But denial has an expiration date, and mine had long passed.

There was something about the quiet of travel that unsettled me at first. Silence had never been my strength. I had spent most of my life inside systems that rewarded motion, productivity, and constant engagement. Stillness felt foreign. Yet over time, that same silence became one of the most restorative elements of the journey. In it, I could finally hear my own thoughts without interruption—and more importantly, I could begin to tell the difference between justification and truth.

The early months were chaotic. I packed without much logic, mixing winter clothes with summer gear, adjusting constantly as climates changed and plans shifted. Looking back, it makes me laugh. One week I was immobilized by depression, and the next I was selling my belongings, closing out a chapter of my life, and driving with no real itinerary beyond the belief that I had to keep moving forward.

There were moments of exhilaration, too—driving long stretches of open road, waking up in unfamiliar cities, and feeling the strange freedom that comes with anonymity. But freedom without intention is just another form of avoidance, and I learned that lesson quickly. I realized, with some discomfort, that I was drinking nearly the same amount on the road as I had been before I left. The setting had changed, but the habit had followed me.

That was a sobering realization.

It forced me to accept that this journey would not work unless I took it seriously—not as an adventure, not as a performance, and not as a way to outrun my past—but as a deliberate act of self-examination. If I was going to continue, I had to engage with the work, not just the movement.

One morning, driving through the Great Smoky Mountains at sunrise, I was struck by how small I felt in the presence of something so vast. Thick fog rested on the peaks like smoke, and for the first time in a long while, I did not feel the need to conquer or control what was in front of me. I simply let it exist. In that moment, something shifted. I realized I did not have to carry every failure, every regret, and every unresolved shame as proof of who I was.

Accountability still mattered. Forgiveness did not mean erasure. But neither did growth require perpetual punishment.

As I continued driving, I found myself laughing out loud—alone in the car—shouting words of understanding into the open air. It wasn't a revelation in the cinematic sense. It was quieter than that. A recognition that humility, not strength, had been missing from my life. That letting go did not mean stopping, and that forgiveness— especially self-forgiveness—was not a reward, but a necessity.

This journey did not make me whole. It did not absolve me. And it did not deliver instant clarity.

What it did was interrupt the cycle.

It gave me space to breathe, to reflect, and to begin understanding the patterns that had shaped me long before I was aware of them. Piece by piece, mile by mile, I started to move away from survival and toward intention. Not perfection. Not resolution. Just forward motion rooted in honesty.

That was enough to keep going.

REFLECTION:

I had no clear direction when I packed my bags for the first time. Within two weeks, I sold nearly everything I owned through a mass Facebook Marketplace sale, put my house on the market, and left town. There is a difference between planning something and actually doing it—once I made the decision to leave, nothing was going to stop me.

Was I prepared to live out of a suitcase for an entire year? No. Was it uncomfortable at first? Absolutely. But I now believe that discomfort was where clarity first began to surface. For most of my life, I had avoided situations that forced me to sit with uncertainty. This journey taught me how to become comfortable being uncomfortable—something I had never truly practiced before.

Even now, when I revisit this chapter, I remember how foreign stillness felt during that time. My instinct was simple: if I just kept moving, things would get better. What I eventually learned, however, was that no amount of distance—not even sixty thousand miles in a single year—can help a person outrun what lives inside them.

CHAPTER 4

Rise Up

As I traveled, I began to understand that the version of myself I had carried for decades was incomplete at best and dishonest at worst. I had believed that longevity in service equaled maturity, that responsibility equaled emotional intelligence, and that endurance equaled love. Those beliefs allowed me to avoid harder truths about my behavior and my character.

I was forced to admit that I had not always been as loving as I thought I was. I had not listened as deeply as I believed. I had not been as emotionally present for my children as I had convinced myself I was. I had often confused leadership with control and provision with connection. These realizations did not arrive gently. They surfaced slowly and persistently, usually when I was alone, with no distractions left to shield me from them.

What humbled me most was recognizing that many of these

criticisms had been voiced by others long before I was ready to hear them. I dismissed them at the time, confident in my self-assessment. It was not until I viewed my life through my own unfiltered lens—without defensiveness—that those words finally made sense.

I did not lose my third marriage all at once. It deteriorated quietly, in stages, while I was busy convincing myself that sacrifice and endurance were the same as presence. I kept promises that mattered on paper—duty locations, career milestones, financial stability—but failed to notice how distance, routine absence, and unresolved resentment were accumulating interest.

For a long time, we functioned well as a unit. Parenting was shared. Decisions were negotiated. Logistics were mastered. We became efficient at survival, especially in environments where nothing stayed fixed for long. That efficiency masked emotional drift. We solved problems, but we did not always tend to wounds.

I told myself that love could be deferred—that proximity could substitute for intimacy when weekends and holidays were all that remained. I underestimated the cost of that assumption.

Over time, what began as compromise hardened into parallel lives, and eventually into silence. By the time the marriage collapsed, the foundation had already been eroding for years.

The end did not only remove a partner. It dismantled the structure I had used to understand myself. Without it, I was left with an identity that had been defined by service, provision, and obligation—none of which could sustain me when the relationship ended.

Leaving did not immediately change my habits. I was still drinking—sometimes just as much as before. The difference was that now the consequences followed me instead of staying contained. The road did not absolve me of responsibility; it amplified it. With no familiar routines and no one to monitor my decline, I was exposed to myself in ways I could no longer ignore.

At first, I rationalized it. I told myself I was decompressing, that I was in transition, that I had earned the right to ease the pain however I could. But deep down, I knew I was repeating a pattern I had already identified as dangerous. The journey was not failing me—I was failing to take it seriously.

That realization marked a shift. If I was going to continue, I had to stop pretending that movement alone was work. Healing demanded intention, not just distance.

In that moment, I decided that this book did not have to document a perfected recovery. It would document a moment when I chose to live. What came after has been uneven, human, and ongoing. I was no longer documenting, observing, and writing for someone else, but in order to set myself free to journey to places I had failed to allow myself to travel emotionally.

REFLECTION:

Hard truths are especially painful when they arrive while you are traveling with no one but yourself. I remember making a list of individuals I believed I had harmed during my most destructive period. For one week on the road, I reached out to each of them. Many told me they understood what I had been going through and offered forgiveness.

While I was asking for their forgiveness, I was also reclaiming a sense of self-worth for myself.

Each conversation helped me take back a small piece of the identity I had lost. This was the point in the journey where I began to recognize—even before I fully acted on it—that I no longer wanted to simply look good. I wanted to actually be good.

There is a difference. One lives in words and appearances. The other lives in feeling and intention. I wanted to feel aligned with who I truly was instead of continuing to perform the version of myself I believed others expected. I wanted to show up honestly, without pretending or apologizing for my growth. That realization felt freeing in the moment, and it continues to shape how I move through life today.

CHAPTER 5

My Own Prison

From a young age, I knew I was different.

While other kids my age were outside playing, immersed in the culture around them or learning how to master the latest video game consoles, I spent most of my time alone. I was quiet, overweight, and awkward in conversation. I gravitated toward silence and order, toward anything that felt predictable in a world that rarely did.

My closest relationship during that time was not with children my own age, but with my grandmother. She worked at a local community center in a predominantly Black neighborhood where kids gathered during the summer while parents worked long hours. My sister and I spent many days there while our mother worked from early morning until dusk.

Even though we didn't live in that neighborhood, we were treated like part of it. Still, I never quite fit. I was known, but not accepted.

Familiar, but never fully included. That sense of being adjacent—but not belonging—followed me everywhere.

At home, things were no easier. Though my mother eventually managed to move us into a stable house in a predominantly white, middle-class neighborhood, stability did not bring connection. Love and affection were inconsistent. I lived between worlds—too different for one, not enough for the other. I learned early how to exist without being fully seen.

My earliest experience with faith came before I had language for it.

I was around five years old when a great-grandparent died. I remember being awakened in the middle of the night by voices moving through the house. Light from the hallway spilled into my bedroom as silhouettes passed by the cracked door. I wasn't afraid. I recognized the voices. I knew the people.

As I lay in bed, frozen, a calm presence filled the room. In one corner, what appeared to be a familiar figure stood looking down at me—physical, yet not. I felt peace instead of fear. I believed the moment was meant to reassure me, to tell me everything would be okay. Then it was gone.

I questioned that memory many times as I grew older. Others dismissed it. But for me, it marked the beginning of a belief that there was something beyond what I could see—something larger than the confusion I lived inside. It was the first time I felt watched over rather than overlooked.

By the time I was twelve, faith had become a refuge.

We rarely attended church as a family before then. My understanding of God did not come from routine or tradition. It came from solitude—from reading the Bible alone, from studying scripture with an intensity that surprised even me. Faith offered structure when nothing else did. It gave language to feelings I could not otherwise express. It gave me a sense of order when my life felt scattered.

The church itself was old, carrying the weight and wear of history. It was there that someone finally took my questions seriously. When I tried to explain the sensations I felt while reading scripture—the burning in my chest, the moments where words came without effort—I was listened to.

I was told I was chosen.

For a child who had never belonged anywhere, that declaration mattered more than I could explain at the time. It wasn't just spiritual affirmation; it was recognition. It was the first time an adult saw something in me and named it as valuable.

I was given passages to study. I would sit quietly, reflect, and then explain what I felt they meant. My answers were met with approval. Over that summer, church became my world. I memorized calls to worship, ceremonies, and rituals. I preached to empty rooms. I married dolls. I counseled action figures. Alone in my room, I felt closer to God than I had ever felt to people.

By the end of that summer, I was placed on the Sunday program. I preached my first sermon from the pulpit as the youngest speaker the congregation had seen. Soon, I was preaching regularly. Invitations followed. I spoke at churches across the city and beyond it. Adults listened. I was taken seriously.

For the first time in my life, I belonged to something larger than myself.

By my mid-teens, I was formally ordained.

Faith had given me purpose. It had given me direction. It had given me a sense of identity at an age when most people are still searching for one. It was not something I questioned then. It was something I trusted completely.

But as I grew older, the world I preached about began to collide with the world I lived in.

I became more aware of poverty, family tension, and contradictions I could not reconcile. The certainty that had once brought comfort began to feel heavy. Passages that once offered reassurance now carried expectation. I began to wonder whether I was living the life I was preaching—or simply living up to what others believed I should be.

I did not lose my faith.

I lost my certainty.

The questions came quietly at first. Then they multiplied. I felt torn between obedience and curiosity, between belief and experience. I prayed not for answers, but for permission—to see the world beyond the boundaries that had once protected me.

Something had to change.

At the time, I did not understand what that change would cost. I only knew that the place where I had first felt at home no longer felt like a place I could stay. Faith had given me my first language for belonging. When that language began to fail me, I did not stop searching for home—I simply learned to look for it elsewhere.

I would not understand the meaning of that shift until much later.

REFLECTION:

As I reflect on those early years, I can see how deeply the search for belonging shaped my identity long before I understood it. Being recognized for my faith gave me a sense of purpose, but it also created expectations I felt responsible for fulfilling. Over time, I learned how easily external validation can become a substitute for internal stability. Understanding that pattern helped me recognize why I often sought affirmation through roles rather than relationships.

Looking back now, I believe there was a form of divine intervention guiding me toward a more honest version of myself. I often thank God for disrupting my path just enough to force me to recalibrate—to slow down, to reflect, and to rebuild a life that feels aligned with who I truly am. For me, that alignment is what peace ultimately means.

CHAPTER 6

Losing My Religion

For most of my life, movement was not an interruption—
it was normal. Stability was measured in adaptability, not
duration. Homes were temporary by design. Relationships were
learned quickly and left just as fast. Over time, I stopped associating
peace with permanence and began associating it with readiness.

That mindset served me professionally. It did not serve me
emotionally.

Constant relocation created a subtle distortion. I learned to equate
usefulness with belonging. If I was needed, I mattered. If I was not,
I drifted. When the uniform came off and the structure disappeared,
there was nothing left to anchor that equation. The very system that
had given me direction had also quietly become the foundation of
my identity.

I had lived inside institutions long enough to mistake discipline for grounding and productivity for purpose. When both vanished at once, the absence felt less like freedom and more like abandonment. The idea of "home" became something I pursued physically because I could not locate it internally. I kept moving, hoping that somewhere along the way I would stumble into a place that felt steady, not realizing that what I lacked was not a location, but an internal anchor.

I didn't notice the silence at first. It arrived gradually, the way absence often does. There was no morning formation. No schedule posted the night before. No one checking whether I had shown up where I was supposed to be. For the first time in more than two decades, no external system cared what time I woke up or where I was going. At first, that felt like freedom. Then it began to feel like something else entirely.

In the Army, structure isn't just order—it's identity. You're told when to eat, when to move, how to dress, where to be, and who you answer to. Over time, you stop thinking of it as control and start thinking of it as safety. Decisions are made for you, and in exchange, you're relieved of the burden of uncertainty. I didn't understand how deeply that rhythm had shaped me until it disappeared. Without it, my days stretched open in ways that unsettled me. Too many choices. Too much quiet. Too much space to hear my own thoughts.

It took time to recognize what I was experiencing. I had seen it before, though I hadn't named it. Men leaving prison after years inside, pausing too long in grocery store aisles. Unsure how to fill an unstructured afternoon. Hesitant in the face of ordinary choices.

The system that had once controlled them had also contained them. When it was gone, so was the map.

I spent half my adult life inside an institution designed to reduce individuality in the name of function. As a Black man, that reality carried additional weight. The Army did not erase race, but it regulated how it could be expressed. There was a uniform way to speak, move, respond, and exist. Compliance was rewarded. Deviation was corrected. Over time, the difference between self-discipline and enforced discipline became difficult to distinguish.

I'm not equating service with incarceration. The reasons are different. The consequences are different. But the process of institutionalization—the long conditioning to external authority, the erosion of personal agency, the quiet surrender of self-direction—can feel strikingly similar, especially when it begins early and extends through adulthood.

Like many men who have spent years in prison, I had been trained to survive inside a system, not to orient myself outside of one. I knew how to follow structure. I knew how to endure it. What I didn't know was how to carry myself without it.

When the institution disappeared, it took parts of me with it. Not my skills, but my bearings. Not my values, but my sense of placement. I had mistaken containment for grounding. I had mistaken order for identity.

I had trained my entire adult life to function within a system. I had not trained myself to exist without one. And in that gap—between structure and self-direction—I began to see how much of my identity had been borrowed from the institution that shaped me. Learning how to live without it would become one of the most difficult transitions of my life.

Only later did I understand that the problem was not movement itself, but what I had never been taught to carry with me.

Before I left, I was assigned multiple therapists and encouraged to engage deeply in treatment. Those professionals were well-intentioned, compassionate, and committed. I do not dismiss their work or their value. For many people, therapy is essential.

For me, something else was required in addition.

What followed was an effort to replace structure with something safer, quieter, and more deliberate. It helped, but it did not resolve what I was struggling to name. There remained questions that could not be answered in controlled environments or structured sessions.

There are truths that surface only in motion. There are questions that do not reveal themselves in familiar surroundings. Being alone in unfamiliar places, stripped of routine and expectation, forced me to confront myself without the framework I had relied on for most of my adult life. Travel did not replace therapy; it complemented what I had not yet been able to access.

Some problems cannot be solved sitting still.

REFLECTION:

When the structure that had guided my adult life disappeared, I expected to feel relief. Instead, I encountered a level of uncertainty I had never experienced before. Looking back, I can see how deeply I had relied on external systems to define my sense of direction. Without them, I struggled—not because I lacked discipline, but because I had never developed an internal framework to replace what had been removed.

That transition forced me to confront an uncomfortable truth: there is a difference between functioning within a system and understanding yourself outside of one. For the first time in my adult life, I had to learn how to carry my own sense of stability rather than depend on something external to provide it.

CHAPTER 7

This Is Why I Love You

This happened before I understood what I was reaching for—before I had any framework for why stillness unsettled me or why silence felt dangerous. I had returned to Kentucky and stepped back into a life that appeared stable on the surface, but the structure that had once contained me was already gone. Without it, my days stretched open in unfamiliar ways, and the restlessness I had carried for years finally had room to surface.

I knew how to perform under pressure. I had spent most of my adult life doing exactly that. What I didn't know—what no institution had ever taught me—was how to be present without a role, or how to exist without needing to be needed.

At the same time, the life I was returning to no longer recognized me. My wife and I were no longer living in the same house. We barely spoke. The kids moved between us on a weekly rotation that felt more like logistics than family life. I had imagined this return as a reset—something familiar I could fall back into. Instead, it felt like stepping into a life that had already learned how to move forward without me.

During the years I had been away, my family had developed their own rhythm. Now I was trying to insert myself into it. Even when I was surrounded by the people I loved most, I felt like a guest. And underneath all of it, my drinking—something I had ignored and minimized for a long time—was no longer subtle.

At the time, I believed I could explain my way out of the damage. I thought I could apologize to my children for being gone so long and convince my soon-to-be ex-wife that my dishonesty and infidelity were the result of loneliness and stress. I told myself that if I could just make people understand why I had done what I'd done, things might soften.

They didn't.

What I couldn't admit yet was that nothing had made me behave the way I had. Not distance. Not pressure. Not alcohol. Every problem I was facing had been shaped by my own choices. I wouldn't fully face that truth for years—but it was already there, waiting.

The house was quiet on the nights the kids weren't home.

Too quiet.

Those nights became permission slips. I drank without pretending.

I poured heavier and faster, telling myself I was unwinding when I was really just trying to disappear. I had no hobbies, no real outlets—nothing to interrupt the hours except alcohol and whatever could distract me long enough to pass out.

After enough bourbon, I would sit on the couch and scroll. Click. Scroll again. Anything to keep my mind occupied until the room went dark.

That's how I found live streaming.

At first, it didn't feel dangerous. It felt alive.

Ordinary people sat in front of cameras, talking to strangers in real time. No scripts. No filters. No expectations. I didn't have to explain myself. I didn't have to be accountable. I could show up exactly as I was—or as something else entirely.

What I didn't realize then was that I wasn't watching connection.

I was watching performance.

And I knew how to perform.

I started spending money in those streams, sending gifts just to hear my name spoken out loud.

When someone laughed at my comments or acknowledged me on screen, it felt like recognition.

It didn't matter that they didn't really know me. In those moments, I felt visible.

Eventually, I turned the camera on myself.

I created a persona—Black Thunda—and built a character that could survive anything. Loud. Confident. Untouchable. The opposite of the man sitting alone in a quiet house.

Streaming became my stage.

The ritual was always the same.

I poured bourbon—straight, no ice—and set it within arm's reach of the camera. I hit "Go Live."

The audience showed up. I drank. They reacted. I drank more. They stayed.

Four hours. Five. Sometimes longer.

The more I drank, the more exaggerated the performance became. I raised my voice. I leaned into conflict. Anger landed better than honesty. Jealousy kept people watching. Arguments stretched into shouting matches that lasted longer than they should have.

The bottle wasn't hiding in the background.

It was part of the show.

Night after night, I performed my addiction for an audience that didn't know they were watching a man disappear in real time. And I mistook views, attention, and chaos for acceptance.

Still, there were real people behind the screens.

Friends. Rivals. Familiar names that returned night after night. That's the reason I titled this chapter This Is Why I Love You. Not because of the platform or the persona, but because of the human moments that slipped through when I wasn't trying so hard.

There were nights when a smile on the screen—brief, unguarded—cut through everything. I remember thinking of the song This Is Why I Love You and how its message captured what I felt in those moments: a brief sense of relief from the noise, not because the pain was gone, but because I didn't feel alone in it.

One person mattered more than I was willing to admit.

She streamed from London. A British accent that pulled me in immediately. Moroccan skin, long dark hair, effortless beauty. At first, I showed up to be loud—to troll, to provoke, to be seen. That was the culture.

But it changed.

I began waking up early just to catch her broadcasts. Adjusting my schedule around her time zone. Learning details about her life. Convincing myself that what I felt was real, even though it lived entirely on a screen.

When I began streaming myself, we sometimes shared the camera. Our banter turned flirtatious. The audience leaned in. I leaned into the role of the hopelessly smitten American across the Atlantic.

And then alcohol did what it always does.

I became jealous. Possessive. If another man drew her attention, I reacted. Streams that once felt playful turned hostile. Arguments escalated. Voices rose. Threats were thrown. What had started as entertainment turned into nightly emotional warfare.

I wasn't connecting anymore.

I was unraveling in public.

Eventually, people drifted away. I turned the camera off for good, exhausted and ashamed.

Months later, still moving without direction and long before the journey became intentional, I went to London.

Not to chase anything.

Not to reclaim anything.

But to face it.

I wasn't drinking the way I had been. I had distance from the persona, from the performance, from the stage. I told her I would be in London around my birthday—the same week as hers. I didn't know if she believed me. I wasn't sure I believed myself.

The day I arrived, I sat at a pub killing time. When she called, I turned the camera just enough for her to see where I was.

It took a moment.

Then it landed.

I was really there.

That night, I dressed differently than I ever had on camera. A pink polo. White jeans. Something softer. I wanted her to meet the man behind the performance.

In the Uber ride to the restaurant, I couldn't stop sweating. My heart raced. Years of anticipation narrowed into a single moment. When the car stopped, the sweating stopped too.

Showtime—without the bottle.

I walked into the room and we locked eyes.

Her friends wasted no time. Question after question. Why was I in London? What did I do? Did I have kids? What about my past relationships? They weren't being cruel—they were being protective. I answered everything honestly.

Eventually, the interrogation ended. We stood side by side. Talked. Laughed. Someone suggested a photo, and only then did we realize we were dressed almost exactly alike.

It felt surreal.

We spent the next few days together—meals, drinks, long conversations. It was easy. Comfortable. And quietly clear. She wasn't ready for anything serious.

Neither was I.

I left London without heartbreak. Without resentment. Without pretending it was something it wasn't. What I carried with me instead was something new: proof that I could step off the stage, put myself back into the world, and sit with uncertainty without reaching for a performance.

That mattered.

It wasn't love.

But it was progress.

REFLECTION:

London was the first destination where the emotional weight I had been carrying didn't feel quite as heavy. I had always wanted to travel to the United Kingdom, so stepping off the plane felt like a dream realized. For the first time on the journey, I was able to breathe and allow myself to simply enjoy where I was instead of constantly revisiting where I had been.

London also marked a significant shift in my mindset. While I was happy to be there, I found myself even more excited about meeting acquaintances I had been streaming with for two years—especially the woman I mentioned earlier in this chapter. That visit became far more meaningful than I expected. It was one of the first moments along the journey when I accepted things for what they were in my life instead of trying to force them into something they were never meant to be. I began to understand that not every connection was meant to lead to a romantic outcome, and for the first time, I allowed that truth to exist without resistance. That acknowledgment marked a turning point. For the first time, I wasn't trying to change what was in front of me—I was learning how to live with it.

CHAPTER 8

Dance With My Father

One of my earliest childhood memories of my father takes place outside a small two-bedroom apartment, in a plastic swimming pool on a hot summer day in the 1980s.

The pool was bright blue, the kind meant for toddlers, barely deep enough to cover my legs. The plastic rim was hot from sitting in the sun. My sister and I played in less than two feet of lukewarm water, splashing and laughing the way children do when they don't yet understand what is missing.

I remember my father being there, watching us.

There was an attentiveness in his presence—the kind you feel when someone is paying attention but not participating. He wasn't far away, but he wasn't close either. It felt as though he was responsible for our safety but disconnected from the moment itself, standing just outside the emotional space we occupied.

Childhood memories are often incomplete or distorted, but I have held tightly to the few I have of my father. There aren't many. Because of that, I replayed them over and over, afraid that if I let them fade, the man himself would disappear completely. The sounds, the heat, the smell of sun-warmed plastic—those details stayed with me long after his presence did.

As a child, I didn't know how to name what I was feeling. I only knew that something about the moment felt unfinished. I was close enough to be seen, but not close enough to be known. That distinction followed me far beyond that summer day.

For a long time, that was all I had of him.

A single afternoon.

A blue plastic pool.

A man standing close enough to supervise, far enough to remain untouched.

As I got older, I returned to that memory often. Not because it was joyful, but because it was one of the only times my father and I occupied the same space long enough for me to study him. I searched his posture, his voice, the tension in his shoulders, hoping to find something that explained where I came from or who I was supposed to become.

What I found instead was distance.

My father carried himself like a man burdened by responsibilities he did not know how to set down. There was a sternness to him, a seriousness that left little room for play or softness. Even then, I sensed that whatever weight he carried did not include us—not fully.

He was present, but he was not available.

I didn't understand that distinction as a child. I only knew that something essential was missing. I was being watched, but not embraced. Protected, but not affirmed. That difference quietly shaped the way I learned to relate to people for years to come.

Children don't just need safety. They need acceptance. Approval. They need to know they are wanted, not merely tolerated. There is an unspoken expectation that a father will provide not only shelter, but connection—a sense of belonging that does not have to be earned.

That expectation went unmet in my life.

I don't remember being taught how to ride a bike.

I don't remember being taught how to fish.

I don't remember being pulled aside and told how to navigate failure, rejection, or fear. What I remember is learning those lessons alone.

The absence of my father did not arrive loudly. It didn't come through dramatic exits or confrontations. It settled in quietly—

through missed moments, unanswered questions, and stories left incomplete. I knew I had siblings, though I could never say with certainty how many. I knew my father had lived a full life before me, though the details were treated as something better left untouched.

Questions about him were often met with silence.

Within my family, the past was guarded. Elders carried their private lives closely, especially when those lives included mistakes. The result was an inherited secrecy that left children like me trying to assemble our origins without the benefit of truth.

That silence followed me into adulthood.

Not knowing where you come from creates a restlessness that is difficult to explain. It leaves you searching for validation in places that can never provide it. For me, that search took the form of achievement. If I could be exceptional—academically, professionally, publicly—then maybe I could quiet the questions I was never allowed to ask.

Perfection became a substitute for belonging.

What I didn't understand for years was that his absence didn't just leave a void—it gave me a role. I learned early that if I made myself useful, I could justify my place. If I became reliable, capable, indispensable, maybe I wouldn't be left again. That instinct followed me into adulthood. It made me successful. It also made me tired in ways I didn't yet know how to name.

It was years later, long after I had built a life that appeared successful from the outside, that a song brought that absence into sharp focus.

Dance With My Father by Luther Vandross came on unexpectedly one day, and it stopped me in my tracks. The song describes a childhood filled with affection, protection, and emotional closeness between father and child—an experience that felt completely foreign to me.

I realized I wasn't grieving a man.

I was grieving an experience.

In a June 2023 episode of The Tamron Hall Show, Richard Marx—who co-wrote the song with Luther Vandross—reflected on its lasting impact. He spoke about fatherhood not as a series of grand gestures, but as a long arc of moments: apologies, failures, lessons, acceptance, and the gradual shift from authority to guidance.

What struck me was the idea that, if a father is fortunate, there comes a time when the work of fatherhood settles. When the steep hills and deep valleys give way to something steadier. Something rooted.

That version of fatherhood felt foreign to me.

This chapter is titled after that song not because it mirrors my experience, but because it highlights the distance between what I longed for and what I received. For years, I wished my father could give me back the time that was lost. Eventually, I understood that

I would have to live without that want.

The cost of his absence showed up in ways I didn't recognize at first—anxiety in unfamiliar spaces, a deep fear of abandonment, a tendency to give everything to everyone, hoping that usefulness would guarantee connection. From the outside, I appeared healthy, successful, whole. Inside, I was exhausted from carrying a need that had never been met.

It took becoming a father myself to fully understand the weight of that absence.

With my children, I made a promise early on: they would never have to question whether they were loved. I would not miss opportunities to show affection, even when it felt uncomfortable. Whatever mistakes I made as a parent, emotional absence would not be one of them.

That promise did not come from anger.

It came from grief.

During my travels—long miles on unfamiliar roads—I began to understand that forgiveness is not a single decision. It happens gradually, in fragments, in moments when the past loosens its grip just enough to allow you to breathe.

Somewhere between quiet mornings and endless stretches of highway, I released the anger I had carried toward my father. Not because his absence no longer mattered, but because it no longer needed to define me.

I don't know the full story of his life. I don't know what resources—emotional or otherwise—he had access to. I can only hope that he did the best he could with what he had. Understanding that did not erase the damage, but it allowed me to set it down.

The deepest wounds are often invisible. They don't announce themselves in ways others can easily recognize. From the outside, I looked whole. Inside, I was still carrying the weight of a child who learned too early how to live without what he needed most.

Forgiveness did not close the wound.

But it allowed it to stop bleeding.

REFLECTION:

For years, I believed that understanding my father's absence would resolve its impact on my life. Over time, I learned that explanation and acceptance are not the same. The questions I carried were not only about him, but about the expectations I had formed in response to what was missing. Recognizing that distinction allowed me to release the constant search for answers that could never fully satisfy what had been lost.

There are still moments when I wonder who my father was as a man, but I no longer allow those thoughts to consume or define me. His absence no longer dictates my emotional state. Instead, I focus on the men who did show up in my life—mentors, leaders, and role models who helped shape me in ways he never could. Over time, I learned to appreciate what I have rather than mourn what I did not, and that shift brought a level of peace I had spent years trying to find.

CHAPTER 9

I Am Not Ok

By the time I reached this point in my life, I understood something I had avoided for years: I did not know what home felt like. I had learned how to function, how to endure, how to belong temporarily—but I had never learned how to rest inside myself or anywhere else.

Everything I understood about stability had been borrowed from institutions, routines, and roles. When those disappeared, so did my sense of grounding. I could explain why that happened. I could trace it back to absence, discipline, and survival. What I could not do was point to a place—physical or internal—that felt like peace.

Knowing that was not the same as resolving it.

For most of my life, movement had been my default response. I left when permanence felt unsafe. I adapted when staying required vulnerability. Change became a skill, not a choice. What I had never done was stop long enough to ask what I was actually moving toward.

That question eventually became impossible to ignore.

As I reflected on my past, I began identifying specific locations tied to unresolved pain—places where something had ended, fractured, or never fully healed. These were not just points on a map. They were emotional markers. Moments where I had learned to leave instead of stay, to endure instead of feel, to keep moving instead of coming home.

I chose to return to those places deliberately—not to relive what had happened, but to confront it directly.

I started calling these stops my healing off-ramps. They were not destinations in the traditional sense, but interruptions—places where the journey slowed long enough for memory and meaning to catch up.

Each off-ramp required honesty. None offered comfort without cost.

When I finally slowed down, I was forced to confront the sheer volume of what I had never processed. My life had moved too fast for reflection. There had been no pause long enough to grieve, to feel, or to reconcile loss. The backlog was overwhelming.

I began mapping the events that had shaped me—not in detail, but in sequence. Each memory carried a place, a season, and an emotional weight I had never fully examined. Seeing them laid out forced me to acknowledge patterns I had spent years avoiding.

The exercise was painful, but clarifying. It showed me where I had been wounded, where I had hardened, and where unresolved grief had followed me forward into new chapters of my life.

Up to this point, my life had been shaped by usefulness. Being needed had become my substitute for belonging. Reliability replaced intimacy. Achievement stood in for connection.

Those patterns earned me success and respect, but they left me exhausted and unanchored.

This was where that way of living had to be interrupted—not explained, not justified, but examined.

Travel, in this context, was not escape. It was a framework—a way to place myself back into environments where I had learned to cope and to ask whether those coping mechanisms still served me. Each mile forward carried the weight of a question I had never answered:

What does home feel like when you are no longer running from yourself?

Without that question, movement had been endless. With it, movement became intentional. This was where the rubber met the road.

I could continue living the way I always had—competent, composed, untethered—or I could begin the work of defining home on my own terms. Not as a place I passed through. Not as a role I performed. But as a state of peace I was willing to build, even if I had never been shown how.

What follows is not a story about travel for its own sake. It is an account of moments where motion gave way to reckoning. Where familiarity was replaced by accountability. Where the search for home became deliberate instead of accidental.

This was the beginning of that work.

REFLECTION:

This was where the real work began.

Along the route, I had already started picking up small pieces of healing simply through conversations and real-life encounters on the road. My healing was not beginning in a circle of strangers exchanging intimate stories—I had already done that. Before retiring from the Army, I had attended three rehabilitation programs.

There is nothing wrong with clinical or substance abuse treatment centers. They serve an important purpose, and they help many people. But at that point in my life, I was not ready to follow a structured plan that I had no role in shaping. From my experience, the programs I participated in focused heavily on making sure patients said the right things and learned the language of recovery, but they often struggled to reach the deeper trauma driving a person's behavior.

I did not believe I was special in any way. But I did take a leap of faith that this journey—this road of redemption—could help recalibrate the destructive patterns that had taken hold of my life and guide me toward something healthier. For the first time, I was not waiting for someone else to show me the way forward. I was beginning to believe that I had to build it myself.

CHAPTER 10

Cranes In The Sky

I had reached the point where understanding my past was no longer enough. I knew where the patterns came from. I could trace the habits, the conditioning, the reasons I moved the way I did through the world. What I did not yet understand was why none of it was working anymore. The answers I had accumulated explained how I got here, but they did not tell me how to live differently.

For a long time, I believed movement itself was productive. If I kept going—physically, professionally, geographically—I told myself I was doing something meaningful. Progress did not always feel good, but it felt safer than stopping. Stopping required a kind of attention I had learned to avoid.

I didn't think of this as avoidance. I thought of it as discipline.

Music accompanied me during that period, not as entertainment, but as regulation. Certain songs articulated what I had not yet given myself permission to say. One in particular stayed with me. Its message centered on the idea that running, traveling, and staying in constant motion could somehow quiet what was happening internally.

Those themes landed hard because they weren't metaphorical to me. They described my strategy exactly. I believed—quietly but firmly—that movement itself was healing. That distance could do the work I was unwilling to face. That if I stayed in motion long enough, clarity would arrive without my having to stop and confront anything directly.

That belief held until it didn't.

Looking back, I can pinpoint when the internal cracks first appeared.

It was 2019. I had just completed my second master's degree. The work was demanding, but the cost showed up elsewhere. I was stressed. I missed my family. I was drinking more than I admitted to myself.

From the outside, my life still looked intact. I was advancing professionally. I was accomplishing what was expected. I was still functioning inside the systems that had always given me direction.

Internally, I was saturated.

While on active duty, my life had never slowed enough to allow for grief or reflection. Loss followed loss without pause. Responsibility stacked on responsibility. I didn't process pain—I deferred it. I told myself I would come back to it later, when things were calmer, when there was room to fall apart.

There was never room.

By 2022, I was retired and suddenly had the time I had always told myself I needed. I thought clarity would follow. Instead, travel became another extension of the same pattern. I told myself I was searching for perspective, but I was still maintaining distance. Each new place brought a brief sense of relief, followed by the same realization: nothing essential had changed. The restlessness returned. The questions followed. The silence grew louder.

Being alone didn't clarify things the way I expected. It removed the structures that had kept me oriented and exposed what I had been carrying underneath them. Without routine or obligation to lean on, I felt the full weight of what I had postponed.

At the same time, personal demands intensified. Milestones arrived with costs that were framed as necessary and routine, but quietly eroded whatever balance I had left. The systems I had relied on were still functioning, but they were no longer containing me the way they once had.

That was how I knew something had shifted.

The tools I had relied on my entire adult life—achievement, endurance, movement—no longer responded when I asked them to work. They didn't fail all at once. They simply stopped providing relief. Forward motion no longer created distance from what I was carrying. It only ensured that I carried it everywhere.

I didn't know what to do with that realization, only that I couldn't unsee it.

Nothing had gone wrong all at once. It had all arrived at the same time.

I hadn't reached clarity.

I hadn't reached peace.

I hadn't figured out what came next.

What I had reached was the end of the belief that movement alone could save me.

That was the beginning of the off-ramps—before I knew what to call them. Before I understood what stopping would require. Before I accepted that staying put, even briefly, would demand more honesty than continuing ever had.

This chapter is not about resolution. It is about recognition—the moment I understood that the road I was on had no exit, and that if I didn't create one intentionally, I would keep moving without ever arriving.

What followed were not answers, but interruptions. Places where forward motion stopped working and I had no choice but to stay with what surfaced.

Each stop was physical. Each one forced something internal to catch up. I didn't recognize them as off-ramps at the time. I only knew that continuing straight ahead was no longer an option. Reflection:

The real first step to healing or treating any addiction in life is when a person stops avoiding, lying, or pretending they don't have a problem. This chapter represents that reckoning on the journey for me. Alcohol and other destructive behaviors were just tools I used to help deny that something deeper was wrong. The real issue was that I was tired. I had been conditioned all my life to keep moving, to push forward no matter what, and never take the time to release the emotional weight that kept me from ever feeling at peace internally.

I was forty-two years old, single, retired, and highly educated. I had no fewer than ten extremely competitive job offers waiting for me—all six-figure positions I could have stepped into immediately after retirement. On the surface, everything looked exactly the way it was supposed to. I had achieved what society tells you success looks like.

But looking back now, I know that if I had taken any one of those jobs, I would have carried the same unresolved pain straight into the next chapter of my life. I would have stayed busy. I would have stayed distracted. And I would have continued to avoid the very thing that was quietly breaking me—myself.

For the first time, I realized that what I truly needed was not another mission, another title, or another achievement. What I needed was stillness. I needed space to sit with the parts of my life I had spent decades outrunning.

For the first time in my life, I understood that healing would not come from finding something new to chase—it would come from finally stopping long enough to face myself.

CHAPTER 11

Memory Lane

An off-ramp doesn't announce itself. There are no signs, no warning lights, no sense of arrival. It appears when forward motion stops working and there is nowhere left to hide. You don't exit cleanly. You drift. You hesitate. You pull off because continuing suddenly costs more than stopping. What makes it heavy isn't the place—it's the moment you realize you can't outrun what's been waiting.

By the beginning of the third month of the journey, movement had lost its authority over me. I was still driving—still covering ground— but the motion no longer carried relief. Summer was approaching quickly, and I had already logged thousands of miles across the Midwest, trusting movement more than direction, staying on the road because it was familiar, because it postponed decisions.

Three months was long enough to believe I was committed—and

long enough to see how easily I could stay in motion indefinitely. The novelty had worn off. The silence had not. What I was carrying hadn't grown lighter just because I kept moving. Distance had changed my surroundings, but it hadn't changed me.

Somewhere along the way, the idea formed without asking permission. If this journey was going to mean anything, I would have to leave the highway and return to places I had learned to outrun. Not to fix them. Not to relive them. But to see whether they still held the power I had assigned to them.

The first of those places was the childhood home I once shared with my biological father, mother, and half-sister. It was the only house that had stayed in my life long enough to feel permanent. And permanence, in my memory, was inseparable from pain.

From the outside, the house had always passed as ordinary. Inside, it never felt like a home.

Whatever existed there was carefully hidden from view. To the world, everything looked intact. To me, the frame was empty.

That small three-bedroom house on Yosemite Drive was where I first learned the cost of wanting something I wasn't given. As a child, I wanted to be close to the only man in my life. I feared him. I loved him. I needed his attention. What I never learned how to ask for—and never received—was his affection.

For years, I tried to understand why my father carried so much anger. I searched for explanations as a child and again as an adult. I still don't have them. What I remember most clearly isn't the anger itself, but the instability—the way my mother, sister, and I moved in and out of that house, never staying long enough to feel settled, never leaving long enough to forget it.

At the time, I didn't know what that kind of instability was doing to me. I only knew how to adapt to it.

Much later, I told myself I wanted to be a different kind of father. I wanted my children to grow up in a home that felt steady, predictable, and safe. I believed intention would be enough. I didn't yet understand how pain left unattended doesn't disappear—it reorganizes, shaping behavior quietly, without asking permission.

This off-ramp had been marked long before I ever named it. Not because it held the most pain, but because it offered the least resistance. It was familiar territory. Avoiding it felt like carrying something unfinished.

When I finally arrived, I parked across the street and stayed in the car.

I didn't prepare myself.

I didn't pray.

I didn't breathe through it.

I just sat there, exposed to whatever might come.

I studied the house in silence. The yard was smaller than I remembered. The shutters were faded and worn. The tree in the front yard— once small enough to climb—had grown tall and uneven. Time had moved forward without consulting my memory.

I waited.

I expected something to happen. I thought the past would rush in, force itself on me, demand attention. I thought I would feel overwhelmed, unsettled, undone.

Nothing came.

The house didn't respond to me at all. From where I sat, it was just a house—aging, quiet, unremarkable. The door that once held so much power over me was only a door now. It didn't recognize me. It didn't demand anything.

What unsettled me most was how little I felt.

Sitting there, I thought about how often I had walked this place in my mind. How memory has a way of drawing us back—not to change anything, but to remind us of what once held weight.

There is a song that speaks to that instinct—the pull to return to the past, hoping that revisiting it might finally bring clarity or closure. For years, I believed that returning carefully enough, or often enough, would eventually give the past the authority to explain itself.

But parked across the street, I understood something different.

Here I was, back down memory lane—and nothing was asking anything of me. The house wasn't holding happiness or pain in reserve. It wasn't holding anything at all. The past hadn't been waiting. It simply no longer lived here.

In that stillness, something became clear. The reckoning I had prepared for wasn't going to happen—not here, not like this. The place I had blamed had already lost its authority over me.

I wasn't the child who had lived there anymore. Whatever pain had once existed behind that door no longer had the ability to reach out and hurt me. Not because it was gone—but because it no longer lived there.

When I drove away, I didn't leave the pain behind. I didn't feel lighter. I didn't feel resolved.

But I did feel awake.

The past no longer needed that address to survive.

REFLECTION:

While writing this chapter, I felt many hidden emotions surface. When I stood in front of that house—the first home I could remember from my childhood—I knew the journey was real. My mission had a purpose, and I was unlocking carefully stored trauma from years past.

From my experience, there is nothing more freeing than facing an emotional obstacle head-on and coming out victorious. For much of my life, childhood visions of that house had haunted me, shaped by the failed promises of what I once believed a functional family should have been. Yet there I was, standing as a grown man, ready to release, grieve, and accept the life I was now taking control of.

I promised myself that I would no longer allow memories from the past to cloud my happiness in the future.

CHAPTER 12

There Goes My Life

Part I

Now that I knew what stopping felt like, I couldn't ignore the cost of never having stopped. I had stood still long enough to recognize when something from my past no longer had authority over me. That realization should have brought relief.

Instead, it unsettled me.

Because once I knew what stopping felt like, I couldn't ignore the question that followed:

Why had I lived so long without it?

The answer didn't live where I was now.

It lived where I first learned that stopping wasn't an option.

I stood on a hilltop outside Ferizaj, in southeastern Kosovo. The night was low and heavy—the kind that presses down rather than opens up. Thick clouds erased the moon and stars. On a clear night, the terrain would have been visible for miles. That night, I could barely see ten feet in front of me.

The darkness felt close.

Not empty—close.

For a moment, I wasn't thinking about exposure or risk. I wasn't thinking about the protective gear stacked beside me or how easily I might have been seen from a distance. I wasn't thinking about mission briefings or rules of engagement.

I was on my knees, staring upward, trying to understand how my life had arrived here so quickly—and without asking.

The moment didn't last.

They never do.

I stood, gathered my equipment, and returned to my guard tower overlooking the same darkness I had just knelt in. My job was simple: stay alert through the night and keep other soldiers safe from anyone who might interfere with our peacekeeping mission.

I remember thinking how strange it was to be standing watch in a country whose name still felt foreign on my tongue. I had been awake for nearly two straight days. My body was exhausted. My uniform was dusty. My face unshaven.

Underneath the fatigue was something heavier—something I couldn't afford to look at directly.

A few days earlier, my firstborn child had been born in Germany.

I didn't know what my daughter looked like. I didn't know how she smelled, whether her eyes resembled mine, or whether she would recognize me when I finally held her. By my estimate, she would be nearly five months old before we returned.

I wondered quietly whether I would make it back alive at all.

For a short stretch of that night, I held onto the good thoughts—pride, responsibility, the idea that somewhere in the world there was a child I had helped bring into existence and that it was now my duty to protect her.

When my shift ended, sleep didn't come.

Silence did.

My mind filled it with images of a baby I had never seen. I imagined holding her. I imagined the sound of her breathing. I imagined the weight of her against my chest.

And beneath all of it was a thought I kept forcing down, even as it pushed back harder.

I didn't know for certain that she was mine.

More than a year earlier—before Kosovo, before deployment, before fatherhood had weight—I had been out with friends in Bamberg. I noticed a young woman standing alone in a phone booth, speaking quietly.

I had recently come out of a short-lived marriage and was still trying to understand how quickly life could change. My friends encouraged me to start dating again, and I approached her without hesitation. There was something about her that felt unfamiliar compared to anyone I had known before—different background, different culture, different life experience.

She told me she was close to my age. She told me her family was Turkish. At the time, I didn't know what that difference would mean. I only knew I was drawn in.

We exchanged numbers and met later that night.

Within a month, I felt the same familiar attachment I had experienced before. I didn't yet know how to measure love. I only knew how quickly I gave it away. Attention felt like connection. Connection felt like commitment. I invested fully before I understood the cost.

When we became intimate, it meant something to me. I believed it meant something to her as well.

But we were both very young, and it didn't take long for the cracks to show.

We began seeing other people.

When she later told me she was pregnant and that the child might be mine, shock was the only thing I could feel clearly.

A few days later, sitting alone in my barracks room, I received a call from one of her friends. She told me she couldn't keep lying anymore. What followed came in pieces, each one tightening the space around me.

There had been an age difference between us that I had not fully understood at the time. She had also been involved with another service member during the same period.

There was a real possibility I wasn't the father.

When I confronted her, she confirmed everything.

I didn't collapse.

I didn't confront anyone else.

I didn't tell many people.

I didn't know how to talk about it without pulling apart something I was already barely holding together.

But I made a decision early—before answers, before proof.

I would stay.

PART II

After traveling through different places in the United States, I began to recognize the pattern of off-ramps for what they were—not stops, but returns in disguise. The weight I was carrying wasn't abstract, and it wasn't new.

It had shape.

Committing to a year on the journey made the next step unavoidable. Germany wasn't a destination I chose so much as the place I hadn't gone back to yet. Whatever I carried into fatherhood began there, and this was the point in the journey where avoiding that origin was no longer an option.

I was already overseas again when these memories began to surface with clarity. Different country. Different language. Different time zone. The distance mattered. Being far enough away from the life I had built finally gave me the space to see how it had been constructed.

I wasn't remembering randomly.

The memories arrived with purpose, lining themselves up now that I understood what an off-ramp was and what it required. Only after stopping did I recognize how long I had lived without the option to.

After making the choice to be a present father—without certainty, without proof—life narrowed into function.

There was no room for hesitation.

No margin for doubt.

Responsibility became the organizing principle around which everything else arranged itself.

During the remainder of the deployment, I moved through my days focused on one thing: getting back to Germany to meet my daughter. The weeks blurred together—missions, rotations, routines. I was tired, but it was a familiar tired, the kind that keeps you upright because it leaves no space for feeling.

When I finally returned, my daughter was already crawling.

I remember holding her for the first time, taking her weight into my arms, feeling something immediate and undeniable. Whatever questions I had been carrying fell quiet.

I loved her.

That was enough to keep moving.

Life quickly settled into repetition—diapers, bottles, baths, short stretches of sleep, long nights, days that looked nearly identical to the ones before them. I learned the rhythm of her breathing and the weight of her body as it grew heavier in my arms.

I showed up every day—not because it felt noble, but because it was required.

Eventually, the question of paternity had to be addressed. I told her mother that regardless of the outcome, I would remain in my daughter's life.

I had already spoken with the other man who could potentially be her biological father. He made it clear he wanted nothing to do with the child.

His absence clarified my own position.

I stayed present.

Because I didn't speak German, I relied on her mother to arrange the paternity test. I remember sitting in a doctor's office as blood was drawn from my arm.

Waiting returned.

Days stretched into weeks.

Weeks into months.

The results never came.

In the meantime, life continued.

We tried to maintain a relationship, but trust had already thinned. I remained steady for my daughter while growing increasingly distant from her mother. I carried resentment quietly, avoided confrontation, and used motion to keep difficult conversations at bay.

Responsibility anchored me.

But it didn't repair what had already fractured.

When a letter finally arrived, it was written entirely in German. At the time, there were no tools to close that gap instantly.

I couldn't read it.

Despite what I already knew about the betrayal, I had no choice but to depend on her honesty in that moment—trusting something I didn't yet know how to question.

She told me it confirmed I was the father.

I believed her.

I wanted to believe her.

I carried that document with me for years, producing it when asked, never questioning what I couldn't understand. Certainty mattered less than action.

I had chosen to show up.

Eventually, our relationship ended.

Even after we separated, I remained present in my daughter's life. I spent my free time with her—shopping, eating out, sitting side by side in ordinary moments that felt small then and heavier now.

When I later tried to formalize custody, another truth surfaced.

The document I had trusted wasn't what I believed it to be.

The realization arrived quietly, long after the choice I had made could be reversed.

By then, it didn't undo anything.

I had already become her father.

Standing in Germany now, decades removed, I walked through spaces that once held the beginning of that life.

I didn't outrun my past.

I gave it structure.

I kept it moving.

What I can see now isn't resolution—but pattern.

How responsibility became both refuge and restraint.

How motion kept me functional while postponing questions that required stillness.

The road didn't straighten here.

It simply widened enough for me to keep going.

Reflection:

Looking back now, I can see just how young I truly was when I first stepped into the responsibilities of adulthood. Commitment, I believed, required certainty—that you were supposed to have everything figured out before taking on the responsibility of someone else's life.

What I eventually learned is that commitment rarely comes with certainty. Most of the time, it comes from simply deciding to show up and do the best you can, even when you are unsure of yourself.

Becoming a father gave my life direction when I needed it most. My daughter became a constant reminder that my choices mattered beyond just me. She brought discipline, focus, and purpose into my daily life. I pushed myself to do better because I wanted her world to be more stable and secure than the one I had experienced growing up.

It was not until I revisited Germany on this journey that I fully realized how deeply committed I had been—even at such a young age—to being the best father I could be.

Responsibility can give a person direction and purpose.

But it can also limit the space needed for self-reflection.

It teaches you how to keep moving forward—even when parts of you are still trying to catch up.

CHAPTER 13

With Arms Wide Open

Part I

There was a quiet satisfaction in the way the journey had been unfolding. Returning to my childhood home had forced me to confront what I had long avoided, and Germany had given me space to practice what I'd learned without asking anything from me in return. Being with my daughter's family allowed me to remain present without bracing for impact. I noticed how much lighter I felt moving through familiar places without the weight I once carried into them. The work I had been doing seemed to hold. I trusted myself more. I trusted the process more. For the first time in a long while, stopping didn't feel like a threat—it felt manageable.

That confidence mattered. I carried it with me as the train moved south.

Nuremberg wasn't a new destination. It was a return. I had lived in many places since leaving Germany—built a career, raised children, and filled years with movement—but Nuremberg was where my life first bent under responsibility I didn't yet understand. It was where adulthood arrived before I had the language for it, where decisions were made faster than wisdom could keep up. Long before this journey had a name, Nuremberg had already taught me how easy it was to leave—and how hard it was to come back.

My son lives there. The city and my son have never existed separately in my mind. Nineteen years had passed since I had last been in Nuremberg, and just as long since I had last seen him. That symmetry isn't poetic—it's damning. I didn't lose track of time. I didn't forget. I carried the knowledge of that distance while continuing to build a life that required constant forward motion. I told myself those realities could coexist. I never tested whether that was true.

In the previous chapter, the reader saw me show up—show effort, go beyond what was required for my daughter. That matters. And it doesn't cancel this. I lived with the awareness that I had been present for one child while absent for another, and there is no moral accounting that balances that ledger. Love extended in one direction does not erase silence in another. I wasn't crushed by it daily—but I was never free of it. I learned how to carry that weight without naming it, how to keep it from interfering with the version of myself I needed to be to survive.

As the train moved closer to Nuremberg, explanations stopped helping.

Until then, stopping had allowed me to remain composed. This time, composure felt brittle. I could feel it thinning.

When the call came, I was on campus at Murray State, killing time between classes, half-listening to the sounds around me. When I heard my son was coming, my body moved before my mind caught up. I stood. I walked. I made calls. My hands shook as I wrote things down. Everything narrowed to departure times and flight numbers. I remember the urgency in my chest—the way it felt to finally have something concrete to act on.

I arrived in Nuremberg the day my son was born. I held him. He was warm and impossibly small. His weight settled into my arms, and something in me relaxed for the first time in months. In that moment, the promise felt complete. I had shown up. I stayed as long as I could. I left believing that mattered more than anything else.

At that age, keeping that promise felt like proof. I remember standing there, holding him, watching his chest rise and fall, telling myself that this was the difference between me and my father. I didn't say it out loud, but I believed it fiercely—that this single act separated us. That whatever happened next, my son would never doubt that I cared.

I didn't yet understand how easily a man can mistake one appearance for a lifetime of being there.

I returned to Murray State after the birth. Life resumed without resistance. My daughter and I fell back into routine. My son and his mother remained in Germany, a continent away. The distance didn't announce itself as a problem—it simply existed.

Life didn't pause. Classes continued. Bills came due. My daughter needed rides, meals, and help with homework. I did what was in front of me. Nothing felt broken. That became its own kind of reassurance.

Routine kept me moving. As long as the days were full, there was no room for questions that didn't have answers. Progress looked like motion. Stopping felt indulgent.

Contact didn't end—it thinned. Calls required planning. Time zones became excuses. Letters waited for better moments. Each delay felt harmless. Each missed connection felt temporary. Weeks passed. Then months.

Later became a place I lived in for years.

As the train pulled into the station, I wasn't returning to Nuremberg for the first time since my son was born. I had come back twice before. None of those visits lasted long enough to change anything, but I clung to them. They were proof, I told myself, that I hadn't vanished.

Standing there now, I knew this return wasn't built on the same logic.

As I reached for my luggage, the confidence I had been carrying faltered. I had learned that stopping could lead somewhere healthier. I believed that. But stepping off this train didn't feel like stopping—it felt like exposure.

I knew things about my son without knowing him. I could picture his face without recognizing his voice. I could imagine his life without being part of it. Photographs had arrived over the years— enough to ensure I wouldn't miss him in a room.

He looked like me.

The resemblance didn't feel like connection.

It felt like evidence.

I stepped off the train without knowing whether the belief I had carried for years would survive the moment—or whether it was about to be tested in ways I could no longer prepare for.

PART II

The Facebook message arrived without ceremony. No greeting. No easing in—just a block of text on a screen. Her name hovered above it—familiar, recognizable, and absent from my life for years. I recognized the profile picture immediately. Time had done its work. The image she chose was unsmiling, her eyes distant, her expression set in a way that suggested long seasons of carrying more than she once expected.

For a moment, I didn't open the message.

I stared at the preview line, aware of how much weight could fit into a few words. When I finally read it, the train station around me faded. The noise thinned. The message wasn't cruel, but it wasn't kind either. It wasn't written to protect me.

It was written to protect her.

She knew I was in Germany. She knew I planned to surprise our adult son. I hadn't contacted her on purpose because I feared this exact response. I was focused on my own healing—so fixed on what I needed that I failed to consider how my actions might land on people who hadn't asked to revisit what I had left behind.

She didn't want to reopen old wounds. She didn't want to place our son in the middle of something that could hurt him in ways I hadn't yet imagined.

For the first time, I understood that my timing—my intention— wasn't neutral.

It carried weight.

It carried risk.

It asked others to absorb consequences I had already walked away from.

What I hadn't allowed myself to consider was how my son had grown up navigating a world without me—a biracial child in a predominantly white society in Germany, trying to understand why he didn't blend in like his friends, why his identity carried questions no one around him could answer.

I knew she had married years after he was born. I knew he had siblings—siblings who didn't look like him. And I had to face the truth that my absence meant more than physical distance. I had given him no avenue to see himself reflected, no Black male presence to help him understand who he was becoming.

He may have carried that loneliness for years.

And here I was, trying to insert myself back into his life on my terms—without his consent, without knowing if he was ready, or if he ever would be.

The words *do not attempt to reach out to our son while you are in Nuremberg* hit like a punch to the face.

Not because they were harsh.

Because they were true.

In that moment, I was forced to confront not only what my absence had done to me, but what it had cost her—and how deeply it had shaped his life.

This off-ramp wasn't about my pain anymore.

It was about recognizing the pain I had left behind.

The message didn't stop me.

It clarified the choice.

For the first time, stepping back didn't feel like retreat.

It felt like responsibility.

Nothing in that moment was resolved.

There was no reunion.

No confrontation.

No release.

Only space.

Uneasy, unfinished, and necessary.

I carried her fear with me. I carried his silence. I carried the understanding that love, when it arrives late, does not get to rewrite the years it missed.

What I had mistaken for a destination revealed itself as a threshold instead.

Whatever came next would require more than intention.

It would require patience, humility, and the willingness to let others arrive in their own time—or not at all.

This part of the journey did not end with answers.

It ended with a door left open—and the quiet realization that opening my arms did not mean anyone was obligated to step into them.

Part III

The reunion I had imagined with my son never came.

This stop didn't offer a happy ending or a clear path back to each other—not this time, not on this visit. I stood there with a choice in front of me, and only one of them felt honest.

I thought I was arriving to close a chapter.

What I found instead was a mirror.

For most of my life, I knew how to avoid that reflection—stay busy, keep moving, don't look too long. It was easier to outrun the truth than to sit still with it.

But this journey had taken away my hiding places.

The sadness sat heavier than I expected.

Standing there without him, I felt the weight of everything that never happened—the calls I didn't make, the moments I missed, the version of myself he never got to know.

For the first time, I didn't try to argue with that reality.

It hurt to admit it.

But the pain felt honest.

Accepting that meant facing the possibility that the cycle hadn't been broken after all.

Not because of fate.

Because of choices I had made years earlier.

In the end, this stop didn't give me the reunion I wanted.

It gave me something harder.

And more honest.

I had to stand in the life I had created and accept it without excuses.

For the first time, I wasn't searching for a perfect ending.

I was learning how to live with the imperfect one I had earned.

And somehow, that felt like the beginning of something more real than closure.

REFLECTION:

This chapter forced me to confront the limits of intention. For years, I believed that simply wanting to repair a relationship would eventually be enough. Over time, I learned that healing requires more than desire—it requires timing, readiness, and the willingness to respect boundaries that cannot be controlled.

That realization changed how I understood both accountability and acceptance. Of all the lessons I gained during this journey, this one cut the deepest. I wanted this outcome more than any other. Yet I came to see that my failed attempt to reconnect was not an ending, but an opportunity—an opportunity to reflect, to forgive, to heal, and to prepare for the day when we might both be ready to reunite.

Man in the Mirror

Leaving Nuremberg without seeing my son didn't feel like an ending. It felt like the start of a conversation I had been avoiding for years—one that had nothing to do with distance, timing, or anyone else's choices.

For the first time, I stopped looking outward for answers and turned inward.

The next stop on this journey wasn't a place.

It was a reflection.

Since the journey began, I had always felt the urge to keep moving. This time, there was nothing pulling me forward. No destination. No memory chasing me down. The road that once felt like a lifeline now felt quiet, as if it had done what it needed to do and stepped out of the way.

I had spent months chasing places tied to my past, thinking one of them would give me the moment that fixed everything. Instead, I found a mirror, and it showed me what had been there all along.

The truth wasn't complicated.

I drank too much.

I pushed people away.

I let anger and shame take the place of patience and presence.

The man I believed I was—a devoted father, a steady brother, a reliable friend—didn't match the man I had become. One by one, relationships faded until the quiet around me started to feel normal.

For twenty-five years, I built a reputation on discipline and reliability. From the outside, I looked stable. Capable. Respected.

But depression and addiction don't care about any of that.

When you're deep enough inside them, survival becomes the only thing that matters. And during that stretch of my life, I was convinced I was alone in a hole I had dug myself.

There was no dramatic turning point waiting for me—just a slow realization that nothing around me was going to change unless I did.

Not the past.

Not other people.

Not the damage that had already been done.

Whatever came next had to start with the way I lived.

There was nothing heroic about it. I was just tired—tired of the drinking, tired of the anger, tired of watching pieces of my life fall away while I told myself I was still in control.

For the first time, I admitted I didn't like who I saw.

That was where the real work started.

There were nights when I prayed for relief. Not for success. Not for recognition. Just for quiet. I asked God to take away the thoughts, the loneliness, the drinking, the shame. I asked for my family back. I asked for peace.

I would sit there in the silence, waiting for some kind of answer.

Nothing came.

Back then, that silence felt like abandonment.

Now I see it differently.

I don't think I was being ignored. I think I was being pushed into a place I had spent my whole life avoiding. I had always stayed busy, kept moving, made myself useful so I wouldn't have to sit with what was really going on inside me.

But this time, there was nowhere to go.

No one to convince.

It was just me, alone with the truth.

And the truth was simple:

Guilt hadn't fixed anything.

It hadn't brought anyone back or repaired what I had broken. It only kept me stuck. At some point, I had to accept that punishing myself wasn't the same as taking responsibility.

What mattered now was what I did next.

For a long time, I blamed circumstances for the pain in my life—distance, bad timing, broken relationships, other people's choices.

But when I finally sat with it, I saw something much simpler.

Most of the damage had my fingerprints on it.

The drinking didn't heal anything. It only added new problems. Every angry word, every night I chose the bottle over a conversation, every time I pushed someone away—it all added up.

That realization didn't crush me.

It gave me direction.

If my choices helped create the distance, then different choices could begin to close it.

Redemption wasn't going to come from a speech or one emotional moment. It was going to come from the slow work of making amends—starting with the man I had to live with every day.

The isolation I stepped into wasn't about hiding.

It was about facing myself honestly so that if I ever asked others for forgiveness, I was doing it as someone who had already begun the work.

I wasn't fully healed.

I wasn't suddenly the man society might expect me to be.

I was still uneven.

Still learning.

But I started to accept that progress mattered more than perfection. I didn't have to fix my whole life at once. I just had to live honestly in the moment I was in.

For the first time, that felt like enough.

Being uneven didn't mean I was broken.

It just meant I was human.

For most of my life, I thought I had to have everything figured out before I could feel okay about myself. I thought growth was supposed to look clean and steady—as if once you learned the lesson, you never slipped again.

But that isn't how it works.

Some days I feel strong and clear. Other days I feel unsure, tired, or out of place.

The difference now is that I don't carry the same shame about it.

I'm not perfect, but I'm being honest about who I am—and that honesty feels like progress.

I don't try to live up to everyone else's expectations anymore.

I spent years chasing titles, roles, and approval, thinking that was where my value came from. But none of that meant much if I couldn't sit alone with myself at the end of the day.

Now I focus on being the man I choose to be when I wake up.

Some days I get it right.

Some days I don't.

But the choices are mine—and so is the life that comes from them.

As long as I can go to bed knowing I didn't pretend to be someone else, I know I'm moving in the right direction.

Because of these lessons, I move through the world differently now.

I'm not reacting the way I used to. I'm not carrying the same anger or confusion into every room I walk into. I understand my own triggers better. I recognize when something is mine to deal with—and when it isn't.

That awareness gives me a kind of freedom I didn't have before this journey.

I'm not perfect, and I don't claim to have everything figured out.

But I'm more emotionally aware than I used to be.

I listen more.

I pause more.

I think about the impact of my choices before I make them.

And for the first time in a long time, I feel like I'm navigating my life instead of just reacting to it.

REFLECTION:

Turning inward revealed how much of my life had been shaped by avoiding uncomfortable truths. Accepting responsibility for my choices did not diminish my sense of self—it clarified it.

Looking back, I see that accountability provided a foundation for change that blame never could. That understanding marked the beginning of a more intentional relationship with myself.

Turning inward revealed how much of my life had been shaped

CHAPTER 15

The House That Built Me

PART I

Toward the end of the journey, I started sleeping later than usual.

At first, I blamed it on the road. Airports disrupt your sense of time. Hotel rooms all feel the same. I was eating whatever was open late—drive-thru windows, random spots in cities where I didn't know anyone. I told myself I was just tired. Anyone moving the way I was would be tired.

But something felt off.

On the flight from Louisville to Columbia, I felt pressure building on my right side. Not sharp—just uncomfortable. I shifted in my seat and ignored it. I've ignored worse. I spent most of my adult life ignoring pain. That's what you do when you believe you're built to endure.

As the plane climbed, the pressure worsened. The higher we went, the tighter it felt—like something inside me was filling up with nowhere to go. I gripped the armrest and stared straight ahead.

No way was I asking for help.

I told myself it was gas. Dehydration. Anything simple. Anything that didn't require admitting I was vulnerable.

When we landed and the cabin pressure changed, the pain eased.

I took that as confirmation that I was right.

The next morning, I walked through the hotel lobby and had to stop halfway across. I was short of breath. My neck was throbbing. I leaned against the wall like I was checking my phone. I still gave my friend the same speech.

"I'm good. Just tired."

He looked at me and said what I didn't want to admit.

"We're not twenty anymore."

The hospital was across the street. I walked over like it was an inconvenience.

Inside the emergency room, I kept repeating it.

"There's nothing wrong with me. Don't I look fine?"

I actually believed that.

They ran tests. Drew blood. Hooked me up to machines. I waited for them to tell me I needed fluids and rest—something small, something manageable.

Instead, the doctor pulled the curtain back and got straight to it.

"You have about a liter and a half of urine backed up in your bladder," he said. "Your kidneys aren't draining. They're close to shutting down. Your heart is retaining fluid because it's trying to compensate. That's why you can't breathe."

Then he said the part that finally cut through my pride.

"You're in a touch-and-go situation."

I remember staring at him and thinking, That can't be right.

I walked in here on my own.

But my body had been shutting down while I was busy telling everyone I was fine.

They inserted a catheter to relieve the pressure. There was nothing noble about it. It was uncomfortable and humbling in a way I wasn't prepared for. Within a short time, I was in an ambulance heading to a larger hospital across town.

By the time I reached the ICU, I wasn't cracking jokes anymore.

Specialists rotated in and out. Words like "critical" and "unstable" were used calmly, which somehow made them worse. They were surprised I had been flying. Surprised I had waited.

Surprised I had been walking around like nothing was wrong.

I wasn't surprised.

I had spent most of my life believing I could outlast anything.

That belief had carried me through deployments, divorce, drinking, regret, and a year of nonstop movement trying to put my life back together.

Now I was lying flat in a hospital bed, machines doing the work my body couldn't keep up with.

For the first time on the journey, I wasn't moving.

And for the first time in a long time, I had to admit something I didn't like:

I had come close to not getting another chance.

PART II

I almost died before I fully understood my own life.

Not in combat.

Not in some dramatic accident.

Not in a way that would have made the news.

In a hospital bed.

Because of years of decisions I thought I was managing.

I had been all over the world. Logged the miles. Revisited the pain. Faced my father's absence, my son's distance, my drinking, my anger, my pride. I thought I was doing the work.

But it wasn't until I was flat on my back—tubes running in and out of me, monitors tracking every breath—that everything came together.

Redemption wasn't out there on the road.

It was in that bed.

Redemption started with me.

For years, I punished myself for the choices I made when I was younger. I replayed them. Second-guessed them. Carried them like proof that I had permanently damaged my own life. I told myself I deserved the distance. The regret. The shame.

Lying there, I realized something simple.

Shame doesn't heal anything.

Beating myself up didn't fix my son's childhood. It didn't undo broken marriages. It didn't restore lost years.

All it did was keep me stuck.

Seeking redemption from myself meant releasing the version of me who didn't know better—without pretending he didn't exist. I made those choices. They shaped my life. But I don't have to keep living as punishment for them.

Redemption also meant changing how I show up.

Not speeches.

Not promises.

Not dramatic apologies.

Behavior.

How I listen.

How I respond.

How I handle conflict.

How I treat the people closest to me.

If I hurt people—and I did—the only honest path forward is to live differently. That's the only apology that lasts.

The year on the road wasn't wasted. Every stop forced me to confront something buried for years.

I forgave my father—not because he earned it, not because it erased what happened, but because I was tired of carrying the weight of his absence into every relationship in my life.

Forgiving him broke something open.

I stopped viewing myself as a victim of generational abandonment and started taking responsibility for how I carried it forward.

My relationship with my son is imperfect. It may always be. Life happened. Distance happened. Silence happened. I cannot rewrite that.

But I no longer punish myself daily for it.

I am available.

When he is ready, I will be there.

Not defensive.

Not demanding.

Not trying to make up for decades in one conversation.

Just present.

That is redemption too.

Throughout my travels, I kept trying to make every place feel like home—hotel rooms, Airbnbs, foreign cities, military barracks. I arranged my things the same way. Created routine wherever I landed. Tried to manufacture familiarity.

It took nearly dying to understand why.

Home was never a location for me.

It was an attempt.

An attempt to create stability where I never had it.

An attempt to build belonging wherever I stood.

An attempt to outrun the feeling that I didn't fully fit anywhere.

In that hospital bed, everything stopped.

No flights to catch.

No destinations to plan.

No movement to hide behind.

Just me.

And for the first time in my life, I didn't feel the urge to run.

I didn't need another country.

I didn't need another achievement.

I didn't need to prove anything to anyone—not my family, not the Army, not the world.

I needed to live.

That was the moment redemption stopped being an idea and became a decision.

I don't know how much time any of us get.

What I know is this:

I almost ran out before I finished the work.

If my body hadn't forced me to stop, I would have kept going—kept traveling, kept reflecting in pieces, kept telling myself I was healing while still avoiding full integration.

Growth you don't apply doesn't save you.

Insight without change doesn't save you.

You don't have unlimited time to fix your life.

Neither did I.

That hospital bed wasn't an interruption.

It was mercy.

And if you're still breathing while reading this, you don't need a medical emergency to start your own redemption.

You just need to decide.

REFLECTION:

Being forced to stop the journey early initially felt like a failure. Looking back now, I recognize that I had pushed my body through a grueling schedule. It was time to allow my body to heal and give my mind space to absorb everything I had experienced.

I no longer try to equate a physical place with the peace I feel within. The journey gave me the opportunity to connect with a sense of home in each moment—both in my past and in my present.

I realized I did not gain lessons only from the past year of travel; life had been teaching me throughout my entire lifetime. The heartaches, betrayals, isolation, abandonment, the highs and lows, the successes, and especially the failures all played a significant role in shaping the man I am today.

CHAPTER 16

Home

When I left the hospital, nothing outside had changed.

The same streets.

The same traffic.

The same people rushing like nothing ever stops.

But I wasn't thinking about the next flight. I wasn't checking timelines or measuring progress. For the first time in a long time, I wasn't trying to go anywhere.

There's a clarity that comes when you realize you almost died.

Not dramatic.

Not loud.

Just steady.

I didn't feel victorious. I didn't feel defeated.

I felt exposed.

Like all the noise I had been hiding behind was gone, and there was nothing left to distract me from myself.

Recovery forced me to sit still. Follow-up appointments replaced boarding passes. Suitcases stayed packed but untouched. My body had limits, and I couldn't negotiate with them.

I had plans.

I had a finish line in my head.

Healing didn't care.

It slowed me down anyway.

And slowing down showed me something I hadn't fully faced.

I had spent most of the journey trying to change.

Change habits.

Change reactions.

Change the man in the mirror.

Underneath all of that was something harder.

Acceptance.

Not the kind that feels good.

The kind that feels final.

I had to accept that my son wasn't ready to meet me in Germany.

Wanting it didn't make it happen.

I had to accept that my father gave what he knew how to give — even if it wasn't what I needed.

I had to accept that the journey ended before I crossed the line I drew for myself.

For years, I thought home was something you could pull up to.

A driveway.

A porch light.

A place where the boxes stayed unpacked and your name stayed on the mailbox.

I thought if I found the right city and stayed long enough, the restlessness would stop.

So I kept moving.

Different states.

Different countries.

Different houses.

Each time telling myself, this one might be it.

I was trying to fix a feeling with an address.

I also believed home depended on perfect people.

If everyone loved correctly, stayed close, said the right things —
then it would feel whole. I didn't know what to do when fathers
failed. When mothers weren't what you imagined. When marriages
cracked. When children built lives that didn't revolve around you.

I mistook imperfection for failure.

When I started writing this book, I knew the song Home by
Daughtry was tied to it.

I remembered the line:

"I'm going home, to the place where I belong…"

I used to hear those words like I was chasing a location — a city, a
house, a version of life that would finally quiet whatever felt unsettled
in me.

After the hospital, I heard them differently.

Home wasn't waiting somewhere.

It was the place I avoided the longest — sitting still with myself and not needing to run.

Redemption wasn't dramatic.

It was daily.

It was deciding I don't have to live as a sentence to my past.

I made choices.

Some cost me.

Some cost other people.

I can't erase them.

But I can decide who I am from here.

Faith is what steadied me when I had nothing left to hold onto. I don't believe it was random that I was forced to stop. I believe I was given time.

And time isn't promised.

If I'm honest, I wrote this because I was tired.

Tired of being misunderstood.

Tired of performing strength.

Tired of carrying stories no one heard all the way through.

I wanted my children to know who their father really is.

I wanted my mother to see that I did not waste my life.

I wanted the people I hurt to see the change — not just hear about it.

Almost dying stripped everything down to one question:

If this ends tomorrow, are you living in a way you can stand behind?

Not in a way that looks good.

Not in a way that impresses anyone.

In a way you can own.

I almost ran out of time before I asked myself that honestly.

You may not get a warning.

You may not get a hospital bed.

But if you are still here — you still have the chance to decide who you are going to be.

That's what this journey gave me.

Not a destination.

A decision.

And I finally made it.

AFTERWORD

Finishing this book felt like an accomplishment.

Not in the way people usually think about accomplishment — not like winning something or reaching a milestone that others can measure.

It felt like finishing a task I had avoided for most of my life.

Sitting here today, two years removed from the actual travel, I realize I had been carrying these stories in pieces. Some of them I understood clearly. Others I kept pushing aside because they were easier to manage when they stayed unspoken. I learned how to function without ever putting everything together in one place.

Writing this book forced me to do exactly that.

It forced me to sit down, stop moving, and look at my life in a way I never had before — not just the parts that made sense, but the parts that didn't. Not just the decisions that worked out, but the ones that left consequences behind.

There were moments when I wanted to step away from writing — or even from sharing this story at all. Not because the writing itself was difficult, but because the honesty required to finish it was something I had never fully practiced.

But I stayed with it.

And finishing it matters to me because this is the first time in my life that my story exists in one place — complete, unfiltered, and no longer carried alone.

That is what this first journey represents.

It is not closure.

It is completion.

It marks the point where I stopped trying to outrun my past and instead chose to understand it clearly enough to move forward without it controlling me.

For most of my life, I believed forward motion alone would solve everything. If I kept moving — working, achieving, adapting — I could outpace whatever I hadn't fully resolved.

What I learned through this process is simpler than that:

You cannot build a stable future on a foundation you have never fully examined.

This book represents that examination.

It is the groundwork.

But groundwork is not the structure.

Understanding where you came from does not tell you how to live where you are now, and it does not determine what you choose to build moving forward.

That is where the next journeys begin.

The second book shifts from understanding the past to learning how to live fully in the present. It focuses on relationships, connection, and what it means to remain emotionally open after spending years protecting yourself through distance and discipline.

Because knowing yourself is only the beginning.

Learning how to live honestly with other people is where real growth happens.

Beyond that comes the final stage: deciding what you want to leave behind — not in terms of achievement or recognition, but in terms of impact. How you show up for others. How you contribute to your community. How you choose to use what you have learned in service of something larger than yourself.

Together, these three journeys reflect a full arc:

Understanding your past.

Living honestly in your present.

Building intentionally for your future.

But beyond the books themselves, there is something even more important to me.

Throughout my life, I have seen how many people carry emotional weight without ever speaking about it openly. They learn how to function, how to provide, and how to appear strong, yet often feel disconnected inside.

Many believe they are the only ones experiencing that.

They are not.

One of the most powerful realizations I had during this journey is how much changes when people are given space to speak honestly about their experiences without fear of judgment.

That realization shaped what comes next for me.

Writing is only one part of this work.

The larger goal is to build a community where people can support one another through their own emotional journeys — not as experts or instructors, but as individuals who understand the value of shared experience.

A place where honesty is valued more than appearance.

Where growth is encouraged without comparison.

Where people know they are not alone.

If you are reading this now, you have already taken part in that process simply by being willing to engage with something real.

This book is not an ending.

It is a starting point.

Because life is not defined by where you began or even by what you have been through.

It is defined by what you decide to do next.

And for the first time in a long time, I am clear about what comes next.

Would you like to join me on this journey?

ABOUT THE AUTHOR

 Wes Lewis is a retired U.S. Army leader, world traveler, and author dedicated to exploring themes of redemption, accountability, and emotional growth. After more than two decades of military service and a lifetime defined by constant movement, he began a personal journey to understand the impact of his past and redefine what it means to find peace.

The Long Journey Home: A Road to Redemption and Acceptance is his first book — a deeply personal reflection on identity, responsibility, and the lifelong search for belonging.

Today, Wes focuses on writing, speaking, and building communities that encourage honest conversations about mental health, personal growth, and life transitions. His work aims to create space for individuals navigating change, healing, and self-discovery.

JOIN THE JOURNEY

If this story resonated with you, the journey does not end here.

Wes Lewis continues to share reflections on growth, healing, and life transitions through his writing and online community. You are invited to join others who are navigating their own paths toward clarity, purpose, and emotional well-being.

To receive future reflections and updates, visit:

https://wes-lewis.kit.com/8050ca388a

You are not alone on this journey.